Alligator to Zorse, of Course!

Julia Lynne Cothran

Illustrated by
Leigh Ellen Stewart

ISBN: 978-1-966615-49-1 (Paperback)
ISBN: 978-1-966615-50-7 (Ebook)

Good River Print And Media

DEDICATION

This book is dedicated to everyone who has taught children.

Other books by Author, Julia Lynne Cothran, and Illustrator, Leigh Ellen Stewart, include:

ACKNOWLEDGEMENTS

Thanks:

- To my brother, Alan, who is guiding me from above.
- To my parents and step-parents, Jane and Charles Jackson and Roy and Diana Cothran, for their encouragement.
- To the illustrator, Leigh Ellen Stewart, and her husband, Mark, for their creativity and friendship.
- To Kristin Jarzab for her suggestions and assistance.
- To Nancy Erickson for her enthusiasm for my books.

Open this book and peek inside.
It's where the funny words reside.

They start with **A** and end with **Z**.
That's the alphabet for you and me.

Some words rhyme, and some have rhythm.
But, all the sentences have alliteration in them.

All of these techniques tend to hold our attention.
Below are two examples about which are mentioned.

Makenzie, the moose, made tracks in the mud, while Hannah,
the horse, ate hay.
The "M" and the "H" are letters used for the skills we'll learn today.

Alan, the **a**lligator, **a**mbled **a**way.

Benny, the bear, blew kisses today.

Carl, the cougar, created a fabulous meal.

Debbie, the **d**ormouse, **d**anced in high heels.

Ella, the elephant, eagerly tried
searching for Fendi, that feisty feline.

Gary, the goat, got gum on his tail.

Hendrix, the hoot owl, hijacked the mail.

Iggy, the iguana, ignored the ghost.

Jake, the jackal, ate jam with his toast.

Kristin, the kangaroo, kept looking for clues.

Lawson, the llama, loaned lotion to Lou,
while Maddox, the mastodon, made mud pies for two.

Natalie, the **n**umbat, **n**ibbled on insects till dawn.

16

Ophelia, the **o**possum, hung **o**ver the lawn.

17

Penny, the **p**enguin, **p**layed **p**ing pong with **P**aul.

Quigley, the quail, quilted a doll.

Riley, the rhinoceros, rode race cars at night.

Suzie, the seahorse, swam with delight.

Toukie, the toucan, took tissues to use.

Urie, the **u**mbrellabird, **un**buckled his shoes.

Vinny, the vulture, viewed his valuables in a vault.
Wally, the walrus, whistled, "It's not my fault!"

Xavier, the **X**-ray Tetra, examined his punch.
Yolanda, the **y**ak, **y**elled the loudest of the bunch,
while **Z**eus, the **z**orse, **z**onked out during lunch!

Did you listen carefully, and did you find
that these colorful characters opened your mind?

26

ABOUT THE AUTHOR

Lynne retired from the Kentucky Public School System after teaching language arts for twenty-eight years at the elementary and middle school levels. She holds a master's in elementary education from Murray State University and a master's in principalship and supervision from Indiana State University.

Her books *Does a Gaggle of Geese Giggle?*, *Collective Nouns Abound!*, and now, *Alligator to Zorse, Of Course!* are all in print. She uses humor and rhyme to inform and entertain readers. She calls it "unintentional learning." The reader absorbs the information through vividly illustrated watercolor paintings and verse. Her joys in life are working with children and animals. She has a dog, Max, and a cat, Fendi.

ABOUT THE ILLUSTRATOR

Leigh Ellen Stewart is an eclectic artist producing works of art with a wide range of subject matter, techniques, and media.

Spiritually blessed and inspired by family and friends, Leigh was first introduced to visual art at an early age and pursued a more formal education with degrees in Art Education from Western Kentucky University. Leigh retired from a rewarding thirty-three-year professional career in the public school system and from a small, family-owned business that specialized in the advancement of works for local and regional artisans. Currently, Leigh focuses on creative time with family and works from home.